T0070341

Rolling Through Teens

MARY SETTLE

authorHOUSE®

AuthorHouse™
1663 Liberty Drive
Bloomington, IN 47403
www.authorhouse.com
Phone: 1 (800) 839-8640

© 2017 Mary Settle. All rights reserved.

No part of this book may be reproduced, stored in a retrieval system, or
transmitted by any means without the written permission of the author.

Published by AuthorHouse   10/27/2017

ISBN: 978-1-5246-8459-4 (sc)
ISBN: 978-1-5246-8458-7 (e)

Library of Congress Control Number: 2017904291

Print information available on the last page.

Any people depicted in stock imagery provided by Thinkstock are models,
and such images are being used for illustrative purposes only.
Certain stock imagery © Thinkstock.

This book is printed on acid-free paper.

Because of the dynamic nature of the Internet, any web addresses or
links contained in this book may have changed since publication and
may no longer be valid. The views expressed in this work are solely those
of the author and do not necessarily reflect the views of the publisher,
and the publisher hereby disclaims any responsibility for them.

Contents

Cries of a Young Girls Heart

Siblings

Livin' the Good Life

Cries of a Young Girls Heart

Longing

Sometimes I reflect on my dreams,
My heart's greatest longings,
My life goals,
And the mountains that intimidate.

Is there a man out there somewhere
Who wants me to snuggle up
And spend the rest of my life in his arms,
Though he knows that he could have a better housewife?

We will wake in each other's arms,
Start breakfast with the munchkins, kiss, straighten the tie,
A reminder that lunch is on the middle shelf,
Cups of juice on the bottom.

And he is off; I am left with the kids.
Will I have a friend who comes for a little while,
So I can let them play in the sun,
Or will I be able to be on my own, like a real adult?

What does it feel like to have another body within you?
Do your hearts beat in rhythm?
Can you sense him or her?
Can you feel the life within?

Pondering these thoughts, I open up to my half.
Well-intentioned, she turns me
To look at my mountains full on
And asks how I'm going to scale them.

Is there a man
Who is willing to take on my differences?
Who will meet the standard I set?
Who is special enough to deal with my downfalls?

How will I move quickly enough
To keep my kids safe?
I will probably be the working mom,
While my husband stays with the kids.

Thoughts keep creeping in,
Whispered so convincingly,
Building mountains between my dreams,
Tall and frightening, but so flimsy.

Will I be able to stand back
And watch my husband take my place
In the lives of my little men
Without having my world crash?

Will my husband be tough enough
To not be irritated by my bed hogging
And loud noises
Late at night?

Will I be able to raise my sweeties
Into godly women?
Will I be able to avoid being the hovering mother
That I loathe in my own mom?

The answer comes from deep inside—
Defiant, painful, absolute,
Too strong to throw, crushing my spirit:
No!

When I marry, if I marry,
He will be as annoyed as my gang.
He won't want to share my bed
For I shall roll him off.

Why would he want a woman
Who needs almost as much care
As the children she bears for him
And will stay like that all his days?

Like He always does,
He grabbed my hand,
Rolled up His sleeves,
And set to straightening me out.

First on our tour,
Go to the wisdom of Daddy.
With the voice he uses when I'm broken,
He gathers the remains of a dream
Shattered on the ground.

A gentle reminder
Of a story I know.
A miracle baby, born to be a shepherd
But dreamed of being a king.

Hated by his brothers, sold into slavery, resisted seduction,
He sank below the bottom rung. His mountains
Scaled high. But what seemingly was a blockade between
dream and reality was the stairwell to his divine destiny.

I know that they will have to pick up
Where I fall short. I know not why,
But I know that somehow these mountains
Are guiding me to my dreams.

Steal My Heart

Why is it that
I know God
And I love Him,
Yet my tongue is a lying one?

Why is it that
I never miss a retreat;
I would die before I missed Bradley,
Yet I go days without my devotionals?

Why is it that
I fantasize about beating up anyone who
Hurts those I love? I like to believe I'm strong,
Yet I cry like a baby.

Why is it that
Everyone says I'm a lover of Christ,
And that's what I yearn to be,
Yet I can stab Him in the back all too easily?

I see my worth on the cross
When they nailed the Lord of all creation,
Bound by unseverable cords of love,
For me He bore sin and death.

I hear over and over in my head
His promises to give me a future and a hope
Of a mansion in the heavens;
That I am in His hands, and all will be okay.

Yet I feel like a failure.
I am a liar; I am selfish.
I fall too much; I am a brat.
I am smart, but I'm stupid.

Oh, Lord, steal my heart again.
Protect it. Break it. Mend it.
Let me hide under Your wing,
Away from the fiery arrows.

Help me to see myself
Washed in the blood.
Fix my eyes on You.
I want to be Your daughter.

Where Are You?

Today I went to our special corner,
Where we spent so many special moments.
But you weren't there.
I called for you, but you didn't come.

What happened, My child?
Why are you still searching, ever seeking
The affection only I can provide
In the arms of man?

It's been so long since I've met you here,
So long since we've laughed these laughs
Or cried these tears.
Since we've dreamed these dreams and talked these talks.

What's going on, My child?
Why are you running, ever running
After other lovers?
Why are you chasing other gods?

I sat down under the tree like I used to.
The grass is as green as I remember.
The flowers as beautiful; the only difference,
My beloved, is you are not with Me.

Where are you, My child?
Why are you lying in another embrace?
Why have you laid down your crown of victory for
Chains of slavery? Why are you leaving Me on the tree?

Did you get My letter? Did you read it? Will you let Me in?
Will you rest in My love? Will you let Me be yours?
Will you be Mine? Will you touch My wounds?
Will you caress My tenderness?

When I see you coming, ever so wearily,
I will run, arms open wide to scoop you up,
And we shall be together
Forever!

Weddings

Girls, we fantasize about our weddings nonstop.
When a friend is engaged, we may wonder,
Am I getting an invite? Do I have the privilege of
Joining in this amazing event?

Most girls are crazy about the dresses,
The hair, the makeup, the jewelry,
The glamor of it all.
All she can think of is cake!

We all are invited to a royal wedding.
The admission is free, paid by the Groom.
The bride is dressed in white, pure and spotless.
Feasting for all; seven-year honeymoon.

The date is soon.

The Prince has been preparing an abode,
And soon the Father will say,
"It's time. Go get your bride,"
And off He'll ride.

Lo! Here He comes in the dead of night.
No one expects Him to come.
She is growing weary of waiting.
Skeptics and scoffers scorn her.

Some say He's not coming.
Others mistake patience for absence.
Those who have knowledge without understanding

Say that we are all the workings of a cosmic mistake.

Nevertheless, He comes, sweeps His bride
Away unto paradise,
Serves the one He found,
Sought, rescued, and bought.

Who could never
Pay back the debt she
Rightfully owes her Lover.
A life for a life won't suffice.

But wait; the party has yet to begin
For after that honeymoon,
He comes back on a white horse,
Fire in His eyes, tattoo on His thigh.

His bride comes, too,
Wearing combat boots
To take revenge on the one who
Tried to separate her and her Husband.

But who is she?
This beautiful bride
Who is much beloved
By this handsome Prince?

She's the woman whose husband walked out;
The teenage boy who's never good enough for his dad.
The baby who is sacrificed to Moloch
Before she had a chance to see outside the womb.

She's the man who is persecuted at work
Because he refused to cheat the old lady.
She's the ones who refuse to conform
To the world's system.

She is me; she is my sisters; she is my brothers.
She is all who call on the name of Jesus Christ.
This is the wedding that you don't want to miss
For anything in the world!

The Black Lamb

A flock of white sheep,
Nibbling on pasture, drinking from still waters,
Totally content under the care and guidance
Of the Shepherd.

His eyes scan them all.
Compassion and wisdom
Reflect in them,
Hovering over each one in turn.

They fall on one little lamb,
A unique one,
Different from all the rest,
Not any more special, not any less valuable.

He sees past the smile on her face
Into the thoughts of her heart,
The tears she forbade,
The worries she buried beneath fear.

He strokes her black fur,
The black fur that sets her apart from others,
Though occasionally despised in her eyes,
A treasure in the curse.

"Why art thou cast down, my little one?
Dost thou not play with the others?"
He knows the answer, and He has known
From the time He made her.

"Master," she replies,
"I knowest where Thou hast taken me.
Thy will is perfect.
It is good.

"But why must I be a black sheep
In a white flock?
My coat is ugly,
And I don't belong."

"Lambie, thou knowest not what words thy
Speakest. Though outwardly thy art black,
Thy heart is whiter than theirs.
Thou wilt understand later."

He takes her apart,
Sets her on the mount,
Where she can see the sea of white,
And gives her the eyes to see what He sees.

Suddenly, the similarities disappear,
And she sees that not a one is complete.
From the oldest to the youngest,
All plagued by insecurities.

Even the bravest has fears.
The most beautiful thinks she is not.
The strongest without Him has naught.
All need the Shepherd.

When Women Wear White

"And the two shall become one,"
The ol' saying went.
And hand in hand,
The two thus were sent.

Into perfect paradise
Slithered deception.
The fruit he made her desire,
A wolf in a snake's skin.

More than two thousand centuries later,
We are still feeling the sting
Of the curse
Placed so long ago.

Eve's curse
Still affects her daughters,
Desiring her man.

So does Adam, his sons,
An irrepressible urge to labor,
Provide for the family.

"I do"
Has been stripped to a shadow of itself.
"Till death do us part"
Is very much lip service.

Young people take the precious gift
They have to be the treasured gem

Of the honeymoon
and squander it for misplaced desire.

Girls with girls,
Boys the same,
Forsaking the natural
And burning with lust.
Church bells rejoicing over this.

But listen carefully, and you can hear
God's heart whispering to His bride,
Beckoning to us, drawing us near,
Holding us close to His side.

Marriage was never meant to just please and fulfill
But rather, accomplish the Father's wonderful duty
To show the Master's will
Of love to you and me.

Listen, if you dare,
And you just might
Discover a mystery too wonderful to bear
When women in simple purity wear white.

Jesus's Holy Name Alone

In a world filled with brokenness,
There is so much pain;
Fulfillment is found
In Jesus's holy name alone.

A beer is chugged,
Bud Light hailed as king,
But nothing will ever heal that wound
Like Jesus's holy name alone.

She gives her all
To a boy just to feel love,
But no love is as sweet
As Jesus's holy name alone.

He squanders his salary
On women, drugs, and parties.
Nothing will satisfy
Except Jesus's holy name alone.

Shivering in a corner, hoping to be invisible,
He nurses new wounds as best as a three-year-old knows.
No one cares that he was born to be abused.
Love can be found only in Jesus's holy name alone.

Everyone needs a Savior,
Someone to save them from themselves.
When my world is falling, I know enough to trust
In Jesus's holy name alone.

Garden of Eden

Every girl is a garden of Eden,
Full of pleasure, goodness, and beauty.
A brook of tenderness flows through
To quench thirsts, provide safety to one heart.

Every son is a leader,
Ready to serve and protect
A garden he can call his own
And to love her all the days of his life.

But into the tranquility of romance
Slithered Deception, hating the girl for her beauty
And the boy for God's image in his soul,
And decided to destroy both in one fell swoop.

She bit of his fruit, and her eyes were opened
To a world of lies, hardship, and pain,
And gave also to her love
Instead of guarding his heart.

She wears a mask of colors
To hide her fears.
The safety, beauty, intimacy the garden once possessed
Has been lost.

But a pretty face does not provide identity.
She craves the boy to be his love,
Her God, lost in the jumble of man-made theology,
Is ever waiting, longing for her to come back to Him.

The boy longs to return to the garden,
To have his share of choice fruits,
Rest in the shade of trust;
God is wanting to bring him to the garden again.

The garden is inhabited by giants,
But the boy doesn't want to take risks on the chance that
In climbing toward the prize, he'll slip
And lose everything he worked so hard for.

She flings wide the gate and tempts him
With treasures more precious than gold.
He reaches his hand in to take what she advertises
Without devotion to the heart handed him.

She thrives on love as artificial as he can hand out.
He eats his fill and leaves,
Just another heart broken in two.
She scoops up what remains and searches for another him.

This is the world we live in,
A battleground, not a garden.
If God's daughters are going to make it in love,
We have to remove our sundresses and don our uniforms.

We are in a war, and we are attacking our fellow warriors,
Making them easy targets for the serpent,
Then wonder why they take us in
And then leave us without a second thought.

Pick up your weapon, Princess,
And fight the good fight until the Captain of our salvation
Sends a prince
To tend your garden of Eden!

Siblings

Two of a Kind

I see you gesturing to me to come,
A wrinkled hand outstretched,
Possibly overladen with jewelry,
Maybe your nails dressed with red or pink.

I kneel in front of you, and our eyes meet.
You wrap my arms around your waist
And kiss my cheek.
Our hearts connect without a single word being uttered.

You sit me down beside you,
And I cuddle up,
Holding you close and listening to your breathing.
Aye-aye, taco! We make seal noises.

I sit in your lap,
Two stubby legs on either side of me.
You wrap your arms around me again,
Refusing to share my attention with another living soul.

Your presence still lingers if not in body,
In memory, in affection, in the imprint you left
On my heart and soul and mind.
Flashbacks of moments haunt my thoughts of you.

I close my eyes, and I can see the pearly gates.
God the Father wraps me in His holy love,
Whispers in my ear, "Well done, good and faithful servant;
Enter the joy of your Lord."

Many old friends to catch up with;
Legends of the Bible everywhere.
But the one who sticks out like none other
Is the one who stole my hand like the old times.

We run in the streets together, both completely healed,
Reckless and carefree.
As we pass, people turn and say,
"There goes two of a kind!"

When You Are Gone

I never knew how much I loved you
Till you were not there
To let me use your legs when mine failed,
To talk when I was on my own.

When you are gone,
The face I grew to know is missing, too.
The hugs that I love disappear,
And the smile that brings joy migrates.

I never knew
How much I loved being around you
Till I discovered life without you
And realized my life needs a brother.

When you are gone,
The face I grew to know is missing, too.
The hugs that I love disappear,
And the smile that brings joy migrates.

Still pondering my dream,
Across the ocean you visited me,
Showed me the light at the end of the tunnel that
Would seem stupid to anybody else but is so dark to me.

When you are gone,
The face I grew to know is missing, too.
The hugs that I love disappear,
And the smile that brings joy migrates.

So far away,
Yet by technologation,
You enter my sacred hideaway
And hang in my holy of holies.

When you are gone,
The face I grew to know is missing, too.
The hugs that I love disappear,
And the smile that brings joy migrates.

All around me are memories of you.
School, hugs make me want a Moosified one.
Church, Bradley, Mexico:
All places your presence lingers.

When you are gone,
The face I grew to know is missing.
The hugs that I love disappear,
And the smile that brings joy migrates.

What a glorious reunion it will be
When at last I'm with you,
And I'm scooped up in a big hug
And we set out to desecrate the other Bradleyians!

When you are gone,
The face I grew to know is missing, too.
The hugs that I love disappear,
And the smile that brings joy migrates.

Siblings

I remember long ago when your head was on my lap,
Lying on the couch, totally relaxed.
As I brushed your hair,
No words were spoken; none were needed.

I remember how close we used to be.
My bed was your five-year-old refuge from nightmares.
You were the friend who stayed back when I couldn't play like the others,
And I yearn to know the man that boy has become.

I remember you
As a young babe, a young girl,
Maturing but still just a little one.
And I'll never get back the years we were separated.

I want more than ever
For the veil to lift
And you to turn to the true Savior
And be ushered into the kingdom.

I want to gather you in my arms and know
That for all eternity,
We shall be a family,
Just like we were long ago.

Moosey

Memories of the brother I no longer know
Float through my mind,
Of the life I wish never to the return to,
But the past I'll never forget.

Spotting among the masses
The familiar poof of hair,
My heart leaped,
And I sped up to meet him.

Climbed that giant mountain
That others trod so easily,
Dodged blankets and minglers alike
And was welcomed wholeheartedly on his blanket.

He greeted me with a hug.
And as we talked, the haunting memories faded
And joy filled me,
Joy that comes only from a big brother.

Then Mr. Chocolate-skin came, and our talk was over.
I decided to sneak away,
Wondering if he'd miss me,
Or if he would even notice my disappearance.

I barely got down one step when like the good big brother
He was, he jumped down beside me
And offered to pack me back to the valley
And my black-and-pink stallion.

As soon as I was back in the saddle,
Before I could ask for an escort to the limousine,
He was stolen again,
And I managed to capture my mother.

I couldn't imagine what I would do if he was gone.
I don't know what I would do if I never met him.
I can't see how he is not annoyed with me once in a while.
But I thank God for placing him in my life.

My Rozay

A slip of paper, two or three,
Pink, blue, a faded memory.
I watch as they fall, mindless of
The weight on my shoulders they carry.

A sleepless night, tear, wondering,
Do you feel it, too? The hurting
To pull you into my strong love,
But to open up, I'm fearing.

If I told you, dear, I love you,
If I told you I need my sissy-poo,
Would you take my hand, and together would we
Bridge the gap between time and space, come what may?
Or would you turn your face away? "No.»
Shake your head and send me out. "Go!"
Will you be my bridesmaid someday, my best friend,
My fondest thought? We can work it out some way.
Or will you be my hottest tears,
Lemon juice in my wounds, confirm the fears?

A voice whispers an emphatic,
"Yes-s-s, move along." Too ecstatic
To tear my heart, dreams apart,
My world turned to senseless static.

"She has a new family now.
Might I ask you where, when, and how
She would find the desire
To join with the life, smell like cow?"

If I told you I want to start anew,
Would you say, "Oh, boo."
My hands trembling, heart racing,
I hesitate before I hit call, ringing.

Mouth dry, I almost hang up
And then you pick up.
Voice cracked, mind blank, I whisper
Your name, and you say, "I'm here."
So long I waited for the day.
I don't know what to say.

Food in mouth, Netflix on the way,
Facebook pops up to say
Someone wishes to speak to me.
Put the spoon down, and pause the animation to see.

My breath caught in my chest.
You want me. I don't care about the rest.
My head is a balloon, spinning on cloud 9.
As long as we have each other, we'll be fine,
So grab my hand and hold tight.
We will be all right.

A slip of paper, two, or three,
Representative of your love in me;
Now that we found each other,
We will be forever together!

Big Bro

The fire crackled.
Wondering if he'd be back
In time to lead me into battle,
So I could lead him to victory.

My hope was granted
For when I thought he wasn't gonna show,
I was with him again,
Climbing Sand Mountain.

His footing was lost.
My heart skipped a beat,
Praying he wouldn't hurt himself
Just for me.

First day of camp,
Disappointed we weren't together
But needed to be with Mom
And follow rules without sense.

First team meeting;
No strong man remembered me.
When we took the oath,
I was too short to reach.

Feeling invisible,
I sought his presence,
The hug that made my heart
Smile once more.

When I'm by his side,
I know that
I'll have a brother
For the rest of my days.

His touch
Soothes my longings
And gives me a minute
Of complete satisfaction.

Big Camo Wheelchair

A cool summer night,
Good country filling the air,
Stars twinkling without a care;
Seems like a perfect time to hold tight.

And take a ride on Sissy's big camo wheelchair.
We can take it slow or zoom faster,
Down through the town and out to the candy store.
As long as I have you, it doesn't matter.
Climb upon my lap, and drive if you want to.
You know you have me to hang onto
'Cause I will never let go of you.

A cry; I reach out to hold you.
You just turn and run to another,
And I blink back many a tear.
The tears that remind me how much
I wanted to be that touch,
Even when I am near.
Our cousin has to come over to watch you for our mother.
Eyes downward turned, upon the earth my toe drew.

All I can do is take you for a ride on Sissy's big camo
wheelchair.
We can take it slow or zoom faster,
Down through the town and out to the candy store.
And when you climb down, I can't help
But sit back and wonder
When you realize what I already know.
Just don't make me let go of you.

In the quiet of the night, something stirred in me,
Reminding me of the simplicity of a child.
I will never teach you about makeup, never drive
You to a date, never walk guns in hand through the wild
To drop an animal or two, or surprise you at school and take
you for girl time. If I were to babysit you, it would be only
because you will not need me, And yet, you still see
Everything I do as right.

Because we can ride on Sissy's big camo wheelchair.
We can take it slow or zoom faster,
Down through the town and out to the candy store.
Get on a chocolate craze.
Long as I have you, it doesn't matter.
Climb upon my lap, and drive if you want to.
And I will never let go of you.

No one can love you like I do.
No one can chase you around the living room,
Volunteer for baby duty long
After my time is done.
Fear I'll wake up and you're gone.
I don't want to go through that again; I'm not that strong.
So instead, let's just vroom
Away together, you and me.

And take a ride on Sissy's big camo wheelchair.
We can take it slow or zoom faster,
Down through the town and out to the candy store.
Go cause a little mayhem somewhere.
Long as I have you, it doesn't matter.
Climb upon my lap, and drive if you want to
'Cause I will never let go of you.

I said let's take a ride on Sissy's big camo wheelchair.
We can take it slow or zoom faster,
Down through the town and out to the candy store.
Drink root-flavored beer straight from the bottle,
Turn the lights down and the TV up
Till you fall asleep on my shoulder.
Get hyped up on sugar, and I'll bring you back to Momma.

Yeah, we can take a ride!

Livin' the Good Life

A Piece of Home

It's a place
Where you are loved,
Not for a color of your skin or the price of your car,
But because you are you, and you are there.

It's a place
Where you are welcomed with open arms
Into a new family,
Instantly.

It's a place
Where once strangers
Are best friends
Quicker than the bat of an eye.

It's not flashy
Like Hollywood,
With bright lights
And a name that is known countrywide.

It is not popular
Like New York City,
With all the hustle and bustle
Of the crowds.

It is not important
Like the White House.
It makes no big decisions;
Nor will it ever make headline news.

It is no tourist attraction.
You will not find it on a map.
All it has is given to it almost entirely
By strangers in another country.

It has a few buildings,
Running water, electricity,
No Internet, no cable, no home phone, but it's warmed
By a love stronger than the wars we fight.

Its occupants
Are as simple and dependent
As their abode.
But don't turn your face away!

The boy in the corner, all by himself,
His body so constricted
He's rolled up tight.
A river of saliva running down continuously.

That girl over yonder
Also has a puddle on her shirt.
She pretends to read,
But you know she can't.

There is a girl who always seems to fade into an inconspicuous
corner; nobody escapes her eagle eye.
Whomever it lands upon has no immunity.
They all fall prey to the beauty of the smile.

Take time to listen,
Listen with your heart.
Listen to the stories they tell,
And you'll never be the same.

Most have been mistreated.
The girl who prefers solitude,
She was chained in a basement like an animal
Because she was different.

Here comes one now.
The one with beauty beyond description
And a face like an angel.
She takes hold of your hand and pulls you away.

She pulls you to the couch
And pulls herself up.
Her legs don't dangle because they won't reach the edge.
Without words, she will flip your world upside down.

The boy with his arm around his buddy.
Come close—I dare you—
And he'll pull you in
For a kiss in your hair.

The boy with the consistent pout and crossed eyes,
Yes, he might be repulsive,
But given the chance,
Even Justin Bieber would lose a gaggle of girls.

Without words, they can give you
The quietest whispers of the glories,
Shouts that ring louder than words
Of the love of the Father.

They force you to look inside yourself
At the ugliness you didn't even know was there.
Look outside yourself
At every time they seek to give, despite their own lack.

Look at the girl with gray hair. Look deeper,
Deeper into her heart, and you'll learn
The true power of prayer, how one woman can fight
Many a war in a country she never set foot in.

The one sitting cross-legged on the floor,
Playing with her hands,
Her mission is to show us tenderness
Rarely felt by humans.

The one who will scoot on her knees
Over to let you brush her hair,
The youngster who quickly reminds you of Hammy.
She will take you back to fond memories of youth.

They are like water in August,
Ice cream in July,
A roaring fire in the midst of snowy winter,
Lights in the dark.

They are a quiet place in a society
That tries to define the meaning of you,
Who you should be, what you're not.
They are a little piece of home.

I Love You

I love you.
Eww, what did you say?
I love you
Each and every day!

I love your smile,
The way your eyes light up.
Just for that, I would run many a mile,
My down-day pick-me-up.

I love you.
Eww, what did you say?
I love you
Each and every day!

I love the things you say,
Harshly honest, smart quips;
Speak your mind, whatever it may,
Sweeter than honey, colder than winter that nips.

I love you.
Eww, what did you say?
I love you
Each and every day!

I love when you throw your arms around me,
A way of asking, "Where ya been?"
One move, my king, your check,
Game o'er, the en'.

I love you.
Eww, what did you say?
I love you
Each and every day!

"You can't tell me what to do!"
"Listen to her, Dude, she is a teacher!"
"Watch it, or I will kiss you!"
"«IN-HU-MANE torture!"

I love you.
Eww, what did you say?
I love you
Each and every day.

God Give Me Eyes

He was always up for a hug,
Greeting with a big smile,
Some random car, rolling down the window,
A familiar voice shouting, "I love you, Steph."

God, give me Your eyes to see
The broken, the wounded family
I pass every day.
God, give me Your heart to break
For the ones day in and day out,
Who stumble along the same path and
Struggle to keep on keeping on.

I join a group gathered, favorite pastime eavesdropping
On war tactics, battle wounds, and tales of victories.
But this one had a free water show,
And the snuggle monster came awake inside me.

God, give me Your eyes to see
Your children crying out for love.
God, give me Your heart to heal
The ones shattering in despair.
God, give me Your arms
To comfort my fellow soldiers,
The ones who are in the heat of the battle.

Finally, I made the connection
And heard their stories
About a man leaving his wife,
About her strength to hold her family together,
A woman I rubbed shoulders with,
Who held herself together when
Her world was falling to pieces,
And her husband, I viewed as da bomb dot com.

God, how many beautiful smiles pass me
That hide the broken, ugly, and hideous?
Cheerful greetings hide the sobs.
It is a masquerade ball
Of joyous celebration and laughing,
Dancing, music, merriment
To cover up the fact that no one is as it would seem.

It is true that I no longer see them as I used to.
She is no longer the beautiful woman.
He is no longer the smiling, favorite hug.
She's the Psalm 31 woman I can only pray to be.
He is a hero, the kind the textbooks don't talk about,
The traitor who abandoned his partner
And yet was brave enough to admit he was wrong.

God, I know that they are everywhere—
A brother in a storm, a sister picking up her broken life,
The shopkeeper I pass every day
Who knows a false image of You, sweet Jesus.

So give me the eyes to see,
God. Give me the heart to understand,
The actions to encourage,
The words to soothe.
God, give me the desire, day by day,
To put on the armor of the Spirit,
So I can be used in the battlefield.

Sonshine

Pulled from a deep sleep by a deeper voice,
Pull away from the companion,
Pull on some shoes, and stumble through the door.
Hot coffee fresh from the microwave,
Steam rising, chasing sleep,
Keys in hand, out the door,
And down the road.
Little voices calling from an imaginary canyon.

Calling me back to where I belong,
Calling me to chase,
To play, to snack,
To love, to live.
Calling me home.

An illuminated screen with blue buttons;
Beep-beep, go the five digits.
Pass the class artwork and wonder if
Miss Steph will ever be on one,
Maybe on a ladybug.
Pop into the office just to say hi
And head to the snacks.
Delighted squeals greet me.

"Yaay, Steph's here!"
One voice preceding a chorus of
Enthusiastic, "Hi, Stephanie!"
Two little munchkins join the welcome wagon,
Happy to see I came home again.

I wondered what I did to deserve a place like this.
Am I just another mouth to feed, another
Body to take care of? I don't take much responsibility.
And then, from the mouths of babes, came the unexpected,
Where once he was poking fun at the weird way I talk,
The next, he slapped his companion's arm and quoted
The line I told him just days before:
"She talks weird because God made her different."

Wondered how many times my Father
Has to teach and reteach this simple and simply
Profound lesson. His strength is in my weakness alone;
His purpose in my uselessness.
My only job is to give my heart, all my love poured out
Into my children and enjoy being home where I belong.

With a squeal they take off, thus the chase is on.
For them, a game of innocence;
Me, a powerful reminder of a truth
Hidden in pages all too often all too dusty.
The adversary has a disadvantage.
He has power; yes, great power.
But he has a leash, and unless taunted,
Can only scatter and scare.

They gather around me,
Nothing but smiles, innocent and pure,
And playful tantalizing followed by squeals
As they squirm out of my arm,
Daring each other to come closer. Yeah, this is home.

I follow the little munchkins
Into their room, and one walks up,
Arms outstretched and eyes expectant.
I can't help but smile as I pick him up.
He cuddles up as I pace the room.
I turn around for a second, and
Half the room is lined up for a turn.
And as soon as I put one down, another jumps in.

Sitting around the tiny table,
My buddy beside me—whoops,
Now he's under the table—
Smiling faces surrounding me.
This is home.

Pastor Butthead is spotted down the hall.
Excited to bug him
And talk, even though I have absolutely nothing to say.
But isn't that what family is?
Those special people
That you love spending time with,
Even if you are doing absolutely
Nothing except sitting by him and listening
To the fellas talk Jesus.

But then he deserves to be pestered.
Yes, even deserves to endure
Being chased down to just hang,
Because, after all, it was his chasing after this girl
That made this home.

Back to the kids.
They want another ride.
News spreads quickly among family,
And everyone wants a ride
On a warm lap.
"My turn!" they cry
As they climb up, one by one,
The rest running right beside.
They hang on the sides and huddle around,
So much I can't move without squishing little toes.

We laugh and squeal.
"Steph, don't eat me." Nonsensical jesting.
"I'm not! I'm going to kiss you!"
They are in so many ways my little brothers and sisters.
This is home.

I finally pull myself away from their sweetness.
Beep-beep, bye.
I hesitate at the door, turn, and head
To see if the Big Boss is still in. I would,
If it weren't for the fear of looking like something else,
Spend all afternoon in his office,
Playing on my iPad and rubbing in my football status.
From my uncle to my favorite butthead,
To Grandma in the kitchen,
Cooking up something delicious,
To every single smile imprinted in my head.
This is home.

P31

Her golden hair
Shimmers in the summer sun.
Her eyes gleam,
Full of life and happiness and Jesus.

She has a way of smiling
That would light up a room,
And the way she holds my hand
Is almost as good as Maria.

I close my eyes, and I can see her,
Lying on some hospital bed once again.
Most would call me crazy, but to me,
That's when she is the most beautiful.

Beautiful because
She never gives up;
Beautiful because
She never gives in.

I've never seen her in a bad mood.
I've never heard her complain.
I've never heard her ask,
"Why me, Lord?"

She always has a smile on her face,
And the source of that smile
Is a spring of joy
Found in her Lord.

Beautiful because
She always has something good to say;
Beautiful because
She's virtuous.

She is the type of woman I want to be.
Refuses to back down from what she thinks.
Her tongue can build you up like a skyscraper
But can be as hard as honey to remove once it sticks.

Lying in that hospital bed,
Her head will turn to you.
Look into her eyes, and all you will see is
Beautiful.

Just a Normal Day

I woke up that day,
Swung my feet to the floor, pulled myself up,
And got ready for school like I did for the past years.
Just a normal day.

He woke up, too,
Stood upon legs he always could depend on,
Went through his routine.
Just a normal day.

It was just a normal day
When Moses encountered the burning bush, too,
When Mary conceived God Himself.
It starts like any other day when the Lord intervenes.

I went to school,
Probably fumed about a couple, thinking
My best friend was my caretaker,
Didn't notice the little things that I should have.

He stood for the last time,
But in the blink of an eye,
His world flipped head over heels,
Never to be the same.

It's just another day
When a warrior is chosen
To encounter the enemy
And achieve victory.

It was just another day
When we became friends.
Sitting on that school bus,
Conversations came so easily.

And I could see what it meant,
Faithfulness and trust in the Father,
A strength I could only hope for,
A light like no other.

It's just another day
When you look in the mirror
And realize your goals and dreams
Are miles away from your true potential.

So thank you
For being the young man you are,
For chasing God with everything,
For being my friend.

You Were There

You were there
When I came home
From my epic adventures.
You were there
To wrap my boo-boos the pirate way.

When my heart was stolen
By the man I'm longing to raise a family with,
Yours was the advice
I should've heeded.

When I was uncertain of his availability,
Yours was the voice
That soothed my heart
And comforted my spirit.

When sissy causes my heart to bleed,
Your hands gather the scattered pieces,
And with words sweetly uttered,
You mend my brokenness.

When I hold your hand,
Nothing ever compares to the joy
That overflows my heart,
And no one shall ever replace you nor be as dear to me.

Raining

Lying awake,
Sleepless,
Needing to hear someone,
Reaching for the phone.

This world has left me lame, weary, and worried.
This heart feels like a boulder, and this mind is racing.

Wondering if you're still up.
What would I do without you?
Hoping you will answer;
Hoping you are there.

This world has left me lame, weary, and worried,
This heart feels like a boulder, and this mind is racing.

Sorry if I woke you.
May I cry on your shoulder?
'Cause I don't know where else to turn.
I'm the happiest when I'm with you.

This world has left me lame, weary, and worried.
This heart feels like a boulder, and this mind is racing.

Thanks, my sweet friend.
Thanks for listening.
Thanks for still loving me,
Even when I'm annoying.

This world has left me lame, weary, and worried.
This heart feels like a boulder, and this mind is racing.

Printed in the United States
By Bookmasters